The United States Presidents

Theodore ROOSEVELT

Tamara L. Britton

Big Buddy Books
An Imprint of Abdo Publishing
abdopublishing.com

abdopublishing.com

Published by Abdo Publishing, a division of ABDO, PO Box 398166, Minneapolis, Minnesota 55439. Copyright © 2017 by Abdo Consulting Group, Inc. International copyrights reserved in all countries. No part of this book may be reproduced in any form without written permission from the publisher. Big Buddy Books™ is a trademark and logo of Abdo Publishing.

Printed in the United States of America, North Mankato, Minnesota
062016
092016

THIS BOOK CONTAINS
RECYCLED MATERIALS

Design: Sarah DeYoung, Mighty Media, Inc.
Production: Mighty Media, Inc.
Editor: Lauren Kukla
Cover Photograph: Alamy
Interior Photographs: AP Images (pp. 9, 11, 19); Corbis (pp. 6, 7, 15, 17, 21, 23, 29);
    Getty Images (pp. 5, 7, 25); iStockphoto (p. 27); Library of Congress (pp. 11, 13)

Cataloging-in-Publication Data

Names: Britton, Tamara L., author.
Title: Theodore Roosevelt / by Tamara L. Britton.
Description: Minneapolis, MN : Abdo Publishing, [2017] | Series: United States
    presidents | Includes bibliographical references and index.
Identifiers: LCCN 2015957558 | ISBN 9781680781168 (lib. bdg.) |
    ISBN 9781680775365 (ebook)
Subjects: LCSH: Roosevelt, Theodore, 1858-1919--Juvenile literature. |
    Presidents--United States--Biography--Juvenile literature. | United States--
    Politics and government--1901-1909--Juvenile literature.
Classification: DDC 973.91/1092 [B]--dc23
LC record available at http://lccn.loc.gov/2015957558

Contents

Theodore Roosevelt 4

Timeline 6

Early Years 8

College Man 10

Assemblyman 12

Family Man 14

Public Service 16

A Rough Rider 18

Vice President 20

President Roosevelt 22

A Second Term 24

Adventurer 28

Office of the President 30

Presidents and Their Terms 34

Glossary 38

Websites 39

Index 40

Theodore Roosevelt

Theodore Roosevelt became the twenty-sixth US president on September 14, 1901. Roosevelt worked to end **corruption**. He tried to make life better for US workers. He also fought to **protect** America's land.

As president, Roosevelt worked for peace in other countries. He fought for Cuba's independence from Spain. He also helped end a war between Russia and Japan. Roosevelt's accomplishments improved the lives of millions of people all over the world.

Timeline

1858

Theodore Roosevelt was born on October 27 in New York City, New York.

1900

Roosevelt became vice president under William McKinley.

1898

Roosevelt was elected governor of New York.

1901

President McKinley died on September 14, and Roosevelt became president.

1904

On November 8, Roosevelt was elected president.

1909

On March 4, William Taft became president. Roosevelt left the White House.

1906

Roosevelt won the **Nobel Peace Prize**.

1919

Theodore Roosevelt died on January 6.

Early Years

Theodore Roosevelt was born on October 27, 1858, in New York City, New York. His parents were Theodore Sr. and Martha. Theodore's parents educated him at home. He also studied with a **tutor**. Theodore hoped to one day attend college at Harvard.

★ FAST FACTS ★

Born: October 27, 1858

Wives: Alice Hathaway Lee (1861–1884), Edith Kermit Carow (1861–1948)

Children: six

Political Party: Republican

Age at Inauguration: 42

Years Served: 1901–1909

Vice President: Charles Fairbanks

Died: January 6, 1919, age 60

As a child, Theodore enjoyed natural history.
He collected insects, mice, snakes, and other animals to study.

College Man

Theodore passed his college entrance tests. In fall 1876, he entered Harvard in Cambridge, Massachusetts. Theodore enjoyed his classes.

In 1878, Theodore Sr. died. Theodore decided to work hard. He wanted to become someone important to honor his father. Not long after, he wrote *Naval History of the War of 1812*.

In 1880, Theodore **graduated** from Harvard. In October, he married Alice Hathaway Lee. Later that same year, Theodore entered law school in New York City.

Theodore (*left*) and Alice (*below*) were married on October 27, 1880. This was Theodore's twenty-second birthday.

Assemblyman

In November 1881, Roosevelt was elected to the New York State **Assembly**. He soon earned respect for his work against **corruption**. Roosevelt was reelected to the assembly in 1882 and 1883.

In 1884, the Roosevelts welcomed a baby girl, named Alice Lee. But just two days after her birth, Alice Roosevelt died. Roosevelt was very sad. When his term in the assembly ended, he left New York for Dakota Territory. Roosevelt's sister took care of his daughter.

Roosevelt worked as a rancher in Dakota Territory. There, he raised cattle. He also hunted birds, rabbits, and grizzly bears.

Family Man

In 1885, Roosevelt returned to New York. There, he built a new home on Long Island. He called it Sagamore Hill. Then, in 1886, he ran for mayor of New York. But, he lost the election.

On December 2 that same year, Roosevelt married Edith Kermit Carow. In spring 1887, the Roosevelts moved into Sagamore Hill. It was a happy home for all who lived there.

★ DID YOU KNOW? ★

President Roosevelt was the first American to win a **Nobel Prize**.

In addition to Alice Lee (*top, center*), the Roosevelts had five more children.

Public Service

In 1889, Roosevelt returned to public service. That year, President Benjamin Harrison made him head of the US **Civil Service Commission**. In this position, Roosevelt fought **corruption**.

Then, in 1895, Roosevelt got a new job. He became head of the New York City Police Department. Again, he fought corruption.

In 1896, Roosevelt worked on William McKinley's campaign for president. McKinley won the election! In 1897, he made Roosevelt assistant **secretary of the navy**.

President McKinley (*left*) and Roosevelt

A Rough Rider

Roosevelt worked hard in his new job. At the time, Cuba wanted to gain independence from Spain. Roosevelt hoped to help the Cubans.

Then, on February 15, 1898, the USS *Maine* exploded in a Cuban harbor. Many Americans blamed Spain. So, the United States went to war against that country.

Roosevelt trained a group of men to fight in Cuba. The men were called the Rough Riders. They won an important battle in Cuba. Roosevelt was a hero!

When the USS *Maine* exploded, 266 lives were lost. The cause of the explosion is still unknown.

Vice President

In fall 1898, Roosevelt was elected as New York's governor. He wanted to help workers. So, he passed laws **protecting** child workers. He also gave state workers an eight-hour workday.

In 1900, President McKinley ran for reelection. Roosevelt was chosen as his **running mate**. McKinley and Roosevelt won!

But only six months later, an **assassin** shot McKinley. He died on September 14, 1901. Roosevelt was **inaugurated** that same day.

In the early 1900s, many children worked to help their families. Often they had little time for school. So, Roosevelt limited the number of hours that children could work.

President Roosevelt

As president, Roosevelt worked to **regulate** big companies and aid workers. He created the Department of **Commerce** and Labor. This helped workers receive fair treatment.

Roosevelt also passed laws to build a new **canal**. It would run through present-day Panama. The canal would make it easier for countries to trade with each other.

SUPREME COURT ★ APPOINTMENTS ★

Oliver Wendell Holmes Jr.: 1902

William R. Day: 1903

William H. Moody: 1906

President Roosevelt rode in a steam shovel during Panama Canal construction.

A Second Term

In 1904, the **Republicans** chose Roosevelt to run for president. Alton Parker was running for the **Democrats**. Roosevelt won! He officially became president on March 4, 1905.

That year, Russia and Japan were at war. President Roosevelt met with Russian and Japanese leaders. He helped them work out their disagreements. In 1906, Roosevelt won the **Nobel Peace Prize** for his efforts.

PRESIDENT ROOSEVELT'S CABINET

First Term
September 14, 1901–March 4, 1905

★ **STATE:** John Hay
★ **TREASURY:** Lyman J. Gage,
  Leslie M. Shaw (from February 1, 1902)
★ **WAR:** Elihu Root,
  William Taft (from February 1, 1904)
★ **NAVY:** John D. Long,
  William Moody (from May 1, 1902),
  Paul Morton (from July 1, 1904)
★ **ATTORNEY GENERAL:** Philander C. Knox,
  William Moody (from July 1, 1904)
★ **INTERIOR:** Ethan A. Hitchcock
★ **AGRICULTURE:** James Wilson
★ **COMMERCE AND LABOR:**
  George B. Cortelyou (from February 16, 1903),
  Victor H. Metcalf (from July 1, 1904)

Second Term
March 4, 1905–March 4, 1909

★ **STATE:** John Hay,
  Elihu Root (from July 19, 1905),
  Robert Bacon (from January 27, 1909)
★ **TREASURY:** Leslie M. Shaw,
  George B. Cortelyou (from March 4, 1907)
★ **WAR:** William Taft,
  Luke E. Wright (from July 1, 1908)
★ **NAVY:** Paul Morton,
  Charles J. Bonaparte (from July 1, 1905),
  Victor H. Metcalf (from December 17, 1906),
  Truman H. Newberry (from December 1, 1908)
★ **ATTORNEY GENERAL:** William Moody Charles,
  J. Bonaparte (from December 17, 1906)
★ **INTERIOR:** Ethan A. Hitchcock,
  James R. Garfield (from March 4, 1907)
★ **AGRICULTURE:** James Wilson
★ **COMMERCE AND LABOR:** Victor H. Metcalf,
  Oscar S. Straus (from December 17, 1906)

Roosevelt (*left*) and Secretary of War William Taft

25

Roosevelt loved being outdoors. So he worked to **protect** land for the future. He created five national parks, 18 national monuments, and 51 wildlife **refuges**. He also created the US Forest Service.

At the end of his term, Roosevelt did not want to run for reelection. In 1908, he **supported** William Taft for president. Taft won the election. On March 4, 1909, Roosevelt left the White House for new adventures.

★ DID YOU KNOW? ★

In 1902, Roosevelt refused to shoot a bear while hunting. The event inspired a shop owner to create a stuffed bear. This is how teddy bears got their name!

Roosevelt made the Grand Canyon a national monument on January 11, 1908.

Adventurer

In 1912, Roosevelt ran for president again. However, he lost the election. Then, in 1914, he traveled to Brazil. There, Roosevelt fell from a boat, cut his leg, and became ill. He never fully got better. On January 6, 1919, Roosevelt died.

As president, Roosevelt worked hard to fight **corruption**. Thanks to him, Americans enjoy millions of acres of **protected** land. People around the world will benefit from Theodore Roosevelt's work far into the future.

In 1912, Roosevelt was part of the new Bull Moose Party. The party got its name when Roosevelt said he felt as strong as a bull moose!

Office of the President

Branches of Government

The US government has three branches. They are the executive, legislative, and judicial branches. Each branch has some power over the others. This is called a system of checks and balances.

★ Executive Branch

The executive branch enforces laws. It is made up of the president, the vice president, and the president's cabinet. The president represents the United States around the world. He or she also signs bills into law and leads the military.

★ Legislative Branch

The legislative branch makes laws, maintains the military, and regulates trade. It also has the power to declare war. This branch includes the Senate and the House of Representatives. Together, these two houses form Congress.

★ Judicial Branch

The judicial branch interprets laws. It is made up of district courts, courts of appeals, and the Supreme Court. District courts try cases. Sometimes people disagree with a trial's outcome. Then he or she may appeal. If a court of appeals supports the ruling, a person may appeal to the Supreme Court.

Qualifications for Office

To be president, a candidate must be at least 35 years old. The person must be a natural-born US citizen. He or she must also have lived in the United States for at least 14 years.

Electoral College

The US presidential election is an indirect election. Voters from each state choose electors. These electors represent their state in the Electoral College. Each elector has one electoral vote. Electors cast their vote for the candidate with the highest number of votes from people in their state. A candidate must receive the majority of Electoral College votes to win.

Term of Office

Each president may be elected to two four-year terms. The presidential election is held on the Tuesday after the first Monday in November. The president is sworn in on January 20 of the following year. At that time, he or she takes the oath of office.
It states:

> I do solemnly swear (or affirm) that I will faithfully execute the office of President of the United States, and will to the best of my ability, preserve, protect and defend the Constitution of the United States.

31

Line of Succession

The Presidential Succession Act of 1947 states who becomes president if the president cannot serve. The vice president is first in the line. Next are the Speaker of the House and the President Pro Tempore of the Senate. It may happen that none of these individuals is able to serve. Then the office falls to the president's cabinet members. They would take office in the order in which each department was created:

Secretary of State

Secretary of the Treasury

Secretary of Defense

Attorney General

Secretary of the Interior

Secretary of Agriculture

Secretary of Commerce

Secretary of Labor

Secretary of Health and Human Services

Secretary of Housing and Urban Development

Secretary of Transportation

Secretary of Energy

Secretary of Education

Secretary of Veterans Affairs

Secretary of Homeland Security

Benefits

★ While in office, the president receives a salary. It is $400,000 per year. He or she lives in the White House. The president also has 24-hour Secret Service protection.

★ The president may travel on a Boeing 747 jet. This special jet is called Air Force One. It can hold 70 passengers. It has kitchens, a dining room, sleeping areas, and more. Air Force One can fly halfway around the world before needing to refuel. It can even refuel in flight!

★ When the president travels by car, he or she uses Cadillac One. It is a Cadillac Deville that has been modified. The car has heavy armor and communications systems. The president may even take Cadillac One along when visiting other countries.

★ The president also travels on a helicopter. It is called Marine One. It may also be taken along when the president visits other countries.

★ Sometimes the president needs to get away with family and friends. Camp David is the official presidential retreat. It is located in Maryland. The US Navy maintains the retreat. The US Marine Corps keeps it secure. The camp offers swimming, tennis, golf, and hiking.

★ When the president leaves office, he or she receives lifetime Secret Service protection. He or she also receives a yearly pension of $203,700. The former president also receives money for office space, supplies, and staff.

33

PRESIDENTS AND THEIR TERMS

PRESIDENT	PARTY	TOOK OFFICE	LEFT OFFICE	TERMS SERVED	VICE PRESIDENT
George Washington	None	April 30, 1789	March 4, 1797	Two	John Adams
John Adams	Federalist	March 4, 1797	March 4, 1801	One	Thomas Jefferson
Thomas Jefferson	Democratic-Republican	March 4, 1801	March 4, 1809	Two	Aaron Burr, George Clinton
James Madison	Democratic-Republican	March 4, 1809	March 4, 1817	Two	George Clinton, Elbridge Gerry
James Monroe	Democratic-Republican	March 4, 1817	March 4, 1825	Two	Daniel D. Tompkins
John Quincy Adams	Democratic-Republican	March 4, 1825	March 4, 1829	One	John C. Calhoun
Andrew Jackson	Democrat	March 4, 1829	March 4, 1837	Two	John C. Calhoun, Martin Van Buren
Martin Van Buren	Democrat	March 4, 1837	March 4, 1841	One	Richard M. Johnson
William H. Harrison	Whig	March 4, 1841	April 4, 1841	Died During First Term	John Tyler
John Tyler	Whig	April 6, 1841	March 4, 1845	Completed Harrison's Term	Office Vacant
James K. Polk	Democrat	March 4, 1845	March 4, 1849	One	George M. Dallas
Zachary Taylor	Whig	March 5, 1849	July 9, 1850	Died During First Term	Millard Fillmore

PRESIDENT	PARTY	TOOK OFFICE	LEFT OFFICE	TERMS SERVED	VICE PRESIDENT
Millard Fillmore	Whig	July 10, 1850	March 4, 1853	Completed Taylor's Term	Office Vacant
Franklin Pierce	Democrat	March 4, 1853	March 4, 1857	One	William R.D. King
James Buchanan	Democrat	March 4, 1857	March 4, 1861	One	John C. Breckinridge
Abraham Lincoln	Republican	March 4, 1861	April 15, 1865	Served One Term, Died During Second Term	Hannibal Hamlin, Andrew Johnson
Andrew Johnson	Democrat	April 15, 1865	March 4, 1869	Completed Lincoln's Second Term	Office Vacant
Ulysses S. Grant	Republican	March 4, 1869	March 4, 1877	Two	Schuyler Colfax, Henry Wilson
Rutherford B. Hayes	Republican	March 3, 1877	March 4, 1881	One	William A. Wheeler
James A. Garfield	Republican	March 4, 1881	September 19, 1881	Died During First Term	Chester Arthur
Chester Arthur	Republican	September 20, 1881	March 4, 1885	Completed Garfield's Term	Office Vacant
Grover Cleveland	Democrat	March 4, 1885	March 4, 1889	One	Thomas A. Hendricks
Benjamin Harrison	Republican	March 4, 1889	March 4, 1893	One	Levi P. Morton
Grover Cleveland	Democrat	March 4, 1893	March 4, 1897	One	Adlai E. Stevenson
William McKinley	Republican	March 4, 1897	September 14, 1901	Served One Term, Died During Second Term	Garret A. Hobart, Theodore Roosevelt

PRESIDENT	PARTY	TOOK OFFICE	LEFT OFFICE	TERMS SERVED	VICE PRESIDENT
Theodore Roosevelt	Republican	September 14, 1901	March 4, 1909	Completed McKinley's Second Term, Served One Term	Office Vacant, Charles Fairbanks
William Taft	Republican	March 4, 1909	March 4, 1913	One	James S. Sherman
Woodrow Wilson	Democrat	March 4, 1913	March 4, 1921	Two	Thomas R. Marshall
Warren G. Harding	Republican	March 4, 1921	August 2, 1923	Died During First Term	Calvin Coolidge
Calvin Coolidge	Republican	August 3, 1923	March 4, 1929	Completed Harding's Term, Served One Term	Office Vacant, Charles Dawes
Herbert Hoover	Republican	March 4, 1929	March 4, 1933	One	Charles Curtis
Franklin D. Roosevelt	Democrat	March 4, 1933	April 12, 1945	Served Three Terms, Died During Fourth Term	John Nance Garner, Henry A. Wallace, Harry S. Truman
Harry S. Truman	Democrat	April 12, 1945	January 20, 1953	Completed Roosevelt's Fourth Term, Served One Term	Office Vacant, Alben Barkley
Dwight D. Eisenhower	Republican	January 20, 1953	January 20, 1961	Two	Richard Nixon
John F. Kennedy	Democrat	January 20, 1961	November 22, 1963	Died During First Term	Lyndon B. Johnson
Lyndon B. Johnson	Democrat	November 22, 1963	January 20, 1969	Completed Kennedy's Term, Served One Term	Office Vacant, Hubert H. Humphrey
Richard Nixon	Republican	January 20, 1969	August 9, 1974	Completed First Term, Resigned During Second Term	Spiro T. Agnew, Gerald Ford

PRESIDENT	PARTY	TOOK OFFICE	LEFT OFFICE	TERMS SERVED	VICE PRESIDENT
Gerald Ford	Republican	August 9, 1974	January 20, 1977	Completed Nixon's Second Term	Nelson A. Rockefeller
Jimmy Carter	Democrat	January 20, 1977	January 20, 1981	One	Walter Mondale
Ronald Reagan	Republican	January 20, 1981	January 20, 1989	Two	George H.W. Bush
George H.W. Bush	Republican	January 20, 1989	January 20, 1993	One	Dan Quayle
Bill Clinton	Democrat	January 20, 1993	January 20, 2001	Two	Al Gore
George W. Bush	Republican	January 20, 2001	January 20, 2009	Two	Dick Cheney
Barack Obama	Democrat	January 20, 2009	January 20, 2017	Two	Joe Biden

"The conservation of natural resources is the fundamental problem. Unless we solve that problem it will avail us little to solve all others." Theodore Roosevelt

★ WRITE TO THE PRESIDENT ★

You may write to the president at:
The White House
1600 Pennsylvania Avenue NW
Washington, DC 20500

You may e-mail the president at:
comments@whitehouse.gov

37

Glossary

assassin—someone who murders an important person by a surprise or secret attack.

assembly—a group that meets to make and discuss laws.

canal—a channel dug across land to connect two bodies of water so ships can pass through.

civil service—the part of the government that is responsible for matters not covered by the military, the courts, or the law.

commerce—the buying and selling of goods, especially in large amounts.

commission—a group of people who meet to solve a particular problem or do certain tasks.

corruption—dishonesty by a public official.

Democrat—a member of the Democratic political party.

graduate (GRA-juh-wayt)—to complete a level of schooling.

inaugurate—to swear into a political office.

Nobel Prize—one of the yearly awards given to people who have made great achievements that improve the world.

protect (pruh-TEHKT)—to guard against harm or danger.

refuge—a place that provides shelter or protection.

regulate—to govern or control.

Republican—a member of the Republican political party.

running mate—someone running for vice president with another person running for president in an election.

secretary of the navy—a member of the president's cabinet who handles organizing and running the US Navy.

support—to believe in or be in favor of something.

tutor (TOO-tuhr)—someone who teaches a student privately.

★ WEBSITES ★

To learn more about the US Presidents, visit **booklinks.abdopublishing.com**. These links are routinely monitored and updated to provide the most current information available.

Index

assistant secretary of the
navy **16, 18**

birth **6, 8**

Bull Moose Party **29**

childhood **8, 9**

Civil Service Commission, US **16**

Dakota Territory **12, 13**

death **7, 8, 28**

Democratic Party **24**

Department of Commerce and
Labor **22**

education **8, 9, 10**

family **8, 10, 11, 12, 14, 15**

Forest Service, US **26**

governor **6, 20, 21**

Harrison, Benjamin **16**

health **28**

inauguration **8, 20**

Maine, USS **18, 19**

McKinley, William **6, 16, 17, 20**

military service **18**

Naval History of the War of 1812 **10**

New York City Police
Department **16**

New York State Assembly **12**

Nobel Peace Prize **7, 14, 24**

Panama Canal **22, 23**

Parker, Alton **24**

Republican Party **8, 24**

Rough Riders **18**

Sagamore Hill **14, 15**

Taft, William **7, 25, 26**